THE **JAMES BACKHOUSE** LECTURES

The lectures were instituted by
Australia Yearly Meeting of the
Religious Society of Friends (Quakers)
on its establishment in 1964.

They are named after James Backhouse who,
with his companion, George Washington
Walker, visited Australia from 1832 to
1838. They travelled widely, but spent
most of their time in Tasmania. It was
through their visit that Quaker Meetings
were first established in Australia.

Coming to Australia under a concern for
the conditions of convicts, the two men
had access to people with authority in
the young colonies, and with influence in
Britain, both in Parliament and in the social
reform movement. In meticulous reports
and personal letters, they made practical
suggestions and urged legislative action on
penal reform, on the rum trade, and on land
rights and the treatment of Aborigines

James Backhouse was a general naturalist
and a botanist. He made careful observations and published full accounts of what
he saw, in addition to encouraging Friends
in the colonies and following the deep
concern that had brought him to Australia.

Australian Friends hope that this series
of Lectures will bring fresh insights into
the Truth, and speak to the needs and
aspirations of Australian Quakerism.
The present lecture was delivered at
the Friends' School on 4 July 2016.

Julian Robertson
Presiding Clerk
Australia Yearly Meeting

© The Religious Society of Friends (Quakers) in Australia, 2016

ISBN 978-0-9923857-6-7

Produced by Australia Yearly Meeting of the Religious Society of
Friends (Quakers) in Australia Incorporated
Download from www.quakers.org.au
or order from http://ipoz.biz/ipstore

2016
THE **JAMES BACKHOUSE** LECTURE

Everyday prophets

MARGERY POST ABBOTT

THE JAMES BACKHOUSE LECTURES

2001 *Reconciling Opposites: Reflections on Peacemaking in South Africa,* Hendrik W van der Merwe

2002 *To Do Justly, and to Love Mercy: Learning from Quaker Service,* Mark Deasey

2003 *Respecting the Rights of Children and Young People: A New Perspective on Quaker Faith and Practice,* Helen Bayes

2004 *Growing Fruitful Friendship: A Garden Walk,* Ute Caspers

2005 *Peace is a Struggle,* David Johnson

2006 *One Heart and a Wrong Spirit: The Religious Society of Friends and Colonial Racism,* Polly O Walker

2007 *Support for Our True Selves: Nurturing the Space Where Leadings Flow,* Jenny Spinks

2008 *Faith, Hope and Doubt in Times of Uncertainty: Combining the Realms of Scientific and Spiritual Inquiry,* George Ellis

2009 *The Quaking Meeting: Transforming Our Selves, Our Meetings and the More-than-human World,* Helen Gould

2010 *Finding our voice: Our truth, community and journey as Australian Young Friends,* Australian Young Friends

2011 *A demanding and uncertain adventure: Exploration of a concern for Earth restoration and how we must live to pass on to our children,* Rosemary Morrow

2012 *From the inside out: Observations on Quaker work at the United Nations,* David Atwood

2013 *A Quaker astonomer reflects: Can a scientist also be religious?* Jocelyn Bell Burnell

2014 *'Our life is love, and peace, and tenderness': Bringing children into the centre of Quaker life and worship,* Tracy Bourne

2015 *'This we can do': Quaker faith in action through the Alternatives to Violence Project,* Sally Herzfeld & Alternatives to Violence Project Members

Front cover: Shoreline
Photo: Margery Abbott

Contents

Acknowledgements

About the author

Introduction

Everyday prophets   2

Turning towards the light   7

Headwinds   18

Finding one's rightful place   25

A community in balance   30

Moving with the headwinds   34

Ministry: Moving before the wind   38

Endnotes   42

Acknowledgments

As is often true for me, writing this Lecture has been a collaborative process. In some ways it began nearly a decade ago when a Friend in Philadelphia approached me and insisted I should write about prophetic ministry. Other obligations meant this did not happen immediately but eventually I began work on a much more comprehensive study of the prophetic ministry among Friends today. Integral to that work were queries sent to many Friends of all traditions who are in the public ministry. Most of the stories in this lecture came from these interviews. Many thanks all those who have honoured me with their stories. I want to thank those who responded to my queries about prophetic ministry and all the many Friends who have read all or parts of this manuscript which I hope one day will be part of a much larger work. My apologies to them if I have misused their words.

I also am deeply indebted to my Anchor Committee, Julie Peyton, Darren Kenworthy and Nancy Richard, and my PEER Group consisting of Ken Jacobsen, Emma Churchman and Allison Randall, all of whom have supported me and prodded me through this work. There are many others who have helped me, reading parts of what I have written and otherwise encouraging me. I will not try to name them all as I'm sure I will miss some, but they all have my thanks, as do the Friends in Australia who have invited me to offer this Backhouse Lecture and guided me through this process.

About the author

Marge Abbott is a member of the Religious Society of Friends and has been clerk of a number of bodies including the Friends Committee on National Legislation (FCNL), the Quaker advocacy lobby in the public interest based in Washington DC. Her monthly meeting has formally minuted its support of her ministry as a writer and teacher on Quaker spirituality and history. Abbott carries concerns both for how we might better articulate our faith today and for reconciliation across the divisions among Friends. These concerns flavour her writings which include *To Be Broken and Tender: A Quaker Theology for Today* and *The Historical Dictionary of the Friends*. Among other actions, her concerns have led her to help develop the Pacific Northwest Quaker Women's Theology conferences which have brought together evangelical and liberal Quakers for over two decades.

Introduction

For many years, one of the unknowns of Quakerism was for me the link between faith and action. For a long time I associated faith with statements of belief and knew that action and justice required putting our feet on the ground and our bodies on the line. While I was uneasy with this dichotomy, and suspected this was a misperception fostered by the North American liberal and academic culture that surrounded me, I could not articulate why being a Friend might be explained in ways other than describing a list of ethical actions, and, in particular, the list that reads 'Simplicity, peace, integrity, community and equality.' Taking an ethical stance, acting on the concern for justice and the yearning for peace, does much to open hearts, but many of us have experienced the reality that some activists get caught in the lure of power and pride, then end up becoming what they were resisting. Friends have always asserted that there is another source of guidance that breaks open new approaches to the ills of the world and fuels the work for which Friends are most known.

Faithfulness to the Inward Guide lifts us free of the desire for personal success, or for revenge, or for control over the world around us. Such faithfulness opens the possibility that we might become, as our spiritual ancestors were, a band of what I have come to call everyday prophets. Everyday prophets are people who listen for the Voice of the Light, who might walk humbly even as they come to speak boldly, following the path of compassion and justice.

One of our great gifts is the potential for each of us to act with divine grace, that we might each be an everyday prophet. As such, we seek to listen on a daily basis for God's guidance. Doing this, we can be faithful prophetic voices in very ordinary ways—be it through prayer, caring for our neighbours, small acts of kindness—even as some of us are called to a larger, radical prophetic vision and voice. We do this best as part of a community that is able to carry a vision of the New Creation, the Kingdom of God, being formed on earth as we remind each other to listen for the movement of the Spirit and be open to a fresh way of being.

Everyday prophets

The world is shifting and changing around us in ways few people anticipated in past centuries or even past decades. As Friends we have inherited the wisdom gained from engaging with a spiritual ecosystem that values compassion and generosity over self-seeking and avarice. We are called to sustain a steady witness and to listen for the creative power that treasures healthy relationships and to follow the Light that shows us justice even in the presence of violence and hatred. Our spiritual ancestors show us the power that comes from day-to-day attention to the still, small voice within that points out God's way. We can each of us be instruments of the divine: everyday prophets who act out of God's power in the ordinary path of life and speak the words the Spirit gives us that offer a vision of hope and a counter to fear.

What is an everyday prophet?
So what is an 'everyday prophet'? I suspect many of us carry an image of what I have come to call the 'radical prophets'—the guys in long, tattered, often dirty robes, with unkempt beards and grey hair, preaching doom and gloom. Their message (at least in my head) is that if we don't change our ways, disaster will fall upon the earth! Claiming to foretell the future is their forte.

While this image is one I have purposefully exaggerated, the reality is that I tend to see prophets as radicals who very publicly proclaim wrong-doing and predict harsh consequences. Certainly we have had many such prophets in our midst as a Religious Society of Friends, starting with George Fox, and carried on with folks such as the abolitionists Isaac Hopper, Lucretia Mott.

More recently in North America we might include George Lakey who works for justice in poor Philadelphia neighbourhoods, or Bayard Rustin with his work on civil rights and work with Martin Luther King, Jr. More recently, in 2015 Jay O'Hara sailed a small boat near a dock preventing a huge coal carrier from unloading for a while. His trial brought much attention to climate change issues. Australia has its own prophets, including James Backhouse and Robert Cock who sought to recompense the aborigines.

More recently, Jo Vallentine has been a prophetic voice in parliament on nuclear disarmament and Susannah Kay Brindle has called for those of Anglo heritage to 'pay the rent' to Aboriginal people for the use of the land under Aboriginal spiritual custodianship as well as other work that helps shift the whole way we view our place on this earth.

But there is another kind of action, a way of life really, that is part of our heritage of believing that each person might directly experience the living Christ and follow that guidance, whether it be by speaking in worship or in their day-to-day actions. One example of this that stands clear in my mind is when I saw Pat and Carol at Northwest Yearly Meeting. This would not seem worth commenting on except for the fact that Pat and Carol are a married lesbian couple, and Northwest Yearly Meeting is an evangelical body whose *Faith and Practice* condemns such lives. Pat and Carol did not carry big signs or confront anyone, they simply were present fully as who they are. Their presence helped break through the harshness and fear that can so easily permeate the discussions about same-sex marriage.

At that same yearly meeting, I saw an evangelical pastor step forward and supportively hold the shoulders of a young gay man as he sought the courage to speak in support of changing the *Faith and Practice*. They were each being what I call 'everyday prophets'—people who listen to the voice of all that is Holy and follow its guidance.

But what if we step back and take another look at what constitutes a prophet. I did this by asking many Friends from our varied traditions and from different continents about prophetic ministry, Friends whose words appear in these pages. These Friends are generally well known in their yearly meetings, or even world-wide, and have a clear sense of having been called to witness to God's work. (As an aside, you will find me sometimes using Christian and 'God' language as that is the language of most Quakers worldwide. Please feel free to translate this in ways that speak to you.)

I was struck deeply by the words of Paul Buckley, an unprogrammed Friend from Ohio, who has published books on William Penn and Elias Hicks. He wrote in response to my queries about prophetic ministry saying:

> Focusing on grand events can distract us from our prophetic callings. I can think of particular times in my life that might qualify—dramatic and exceptional events during which I felt as if carried along in the hand of God—but I hesitate to single these out as prophetic ministry. Pulling these instances out implicitly labels them as special or unique. It sets them apart from 'normal life.'[1]

Let me pause here and take note of the way in which Buckley links the 'prophetic' and 'normal life'. He begins to open us up to considering that being prophetic might be something available to all of us. So what does he mean by prophetic ministry? He goes on to say:

> To me, it is essential we not separate prophetic ministry as something that happens episodically or only to certain individuals. Within our tradition, I believe true prophetic ministry is an attitude toward life that produces a renewed state of being. It is the belief we can act at all times under divine guidance. When we are in this condition, every aspect of our lives has the potential to be ministry and each act, however small, can be prophetic …

God in everyone, everyday

Friends have a tradition of pointing to 'that of God in everyone.' Paul Buckley's words affirm that divine spark in each being and expand what that might mean. To see that of God in everyone is not just about respecting each individual, each being on this earth. It is also about each of us knowing that spark within and noticing what the Inward Light is illuminating in our hearts. It is about paying attention when the Inward Guide tells me to act, or gives me words to share. This may be in a public venue, or, as is more often the case, in small groups, in our Meeting communities, in our families, in the places where we work.

The message, in contrast to that of the radical prophet, is rarely earth-shaking in an obvious way, but it may be a simple word that changes someone's day or their life.

I see this in simple examples in my own life such as the time I had an unexpected impulse to call a friend, only to find that she was in tears, totally distraught but unable to reach out. Another time, I had clarity even before I was asked, that it was my time to be clerk of our Monthly Meeting, which was going through a painful struggle over same-sex marriage. Yet another time, when I was asked to speak at Baltimore Yearly Meeting, Julie Peyton, member of Northwest Yearly Meeting of Friends Church and convenor of my Anchor Committee, listened to the Guide then simply and quietly stepped forward to accompany me.

In another instance, the clerk of our Meeting was contacted by neighbours about homeless people sleeping on our doorstep. As she worked with them, she always let us know it was Tony and Sandy she was working with as she sought to find them food and other services. She never dismissed them as 'those homeless people' or otherwise demeaned them. Perhaps in each case it was simply the circumstances, or perhaps it was a beckoning of the Inward Guide that offered such clarity.

If, as I believe, the seed of the prophetic calling grows as we listen daily or even minute by minute for the movement of the Spirit and are faithful in responding, then such actions might be ordinary more often than they are grand.

It takes practice to develop the skill of listening with an inward ear and coming to recognise the taste and colour of all that is holy. I recall being taken aback when I learned that young hawks will often totally miss striking their prey—somehow I thought that was an inborn trait they had from birth. If hawks must practise coordinating their sharp eyesight, their great speed and powerful wings, how much more so for us to undergo a period of trial and failure before gaining any proficiency in the inward life.

Paul Buckley reminds us of the need to nurture the prophetic gift by using a metaphor from American baseball:

> Like the harmony it leads us to live in and into, prophetic ministry is what we do now and work to get better at later. Even for a natural slugger, the difference between home runs and strike-outs is day-by-day batting practice to develop talent and hone skills. Just as with any ability, each time we start where we are and build on it. If I strike out, there will be another at bat coming.

How then might I delineate the nature of an everyday prophet?*

---

* My understanding owes much to the late Bill Taber, a Conservative Friend whose writing, *The Prophetic Stream* (Pendle Hill Pamphlet #256, 1984), has been invaluable. I also am thankful to Brian Drayton, Marian McNaughton, and Lloyd Lee Wilson.

- Above all, such a person is one who listens inwardly and has learned to distinguish the voice of the Spirit, the presence of Christ, from their own desires or self-will, the pressures of the surrounding culture and the need to win approval from those around them.

- Secondly, prophetic ministry requires obedience to that Inward Guide. Prophets are those who recognise what they are called of God to do and who act on this, living as closely as they can to the call expressed in Micah 6:8 to act justly, love mercy, and walk humbly with God.

- Next, a person conscious of the Inward Teacher can see the world around them with eyes that penetrate beyond the surface meanings and cut through the distortions which too often govern life. This person might be able to see unarticulated personal need and a simple, quiet action which makes life better for someone. Or they recognise the consequences of events or words and issue warnings, urging timely change. Such individuals can study our tradition and its ensuing rituals bringing an awareness of where the Life remains as well as seeing what is deadening then naming ways Life might be set free.

This prophetic way of life is a gift that the Eternal seems to offer each of us, yet to accept and fulfill this gift takes attention and practice. Paul Buckley likened this to baseball batting practice. I find resonance with learning how to set the sails as the wind changes. Both these skills take patience and exist embedded in community. Other practitioners are invaluable in helping set parameters, in offering guidance and in providing perspective.

Turning toward the light

In 1750, Samuel Bownas reported how, as a young adult Friend, he would dutifully attend worship every Sunday with his parents and siblings. It was not a particularly edifying experience for him. I can imagine him napping a bit, or wondering about lunch, planning to meet up with friends or keeping an eye on an attractive young woman, or whatever was part of his life at the time. He described himself as 'devoted to pleasure'. One First Day, as he sat in the meetinghouse, there was a visiting Friend who stood and began to speak. As Ann Wilson preached she looked straight at him, pointing. 'A traditional Quaker, thou comest to meeting as thou went from it (the last time) and goes from it as thou came to it, but art no better for thy coming: what wilt thou do in the end?'[2]

These words of Ann Wilson, which shattered Samuel's comfort, feel so alive for me today as I ask myself: How did being in worship change me? How did it bring me more fully into the Ecosystem of Ministry? Am I living in even a tiny way a life more consistent with being part of the New Creation?

Ann Wilson's language might seem alien to some today, but the message was rooted in early Quaker knowledge of the working of the Inward Light. Today we often reference 'holding someone in the Light' as a way of praying for their comfort and well-being. I recall being taken strongly aback one day in worship as I came to experience the Light, not as this benign, gentle warmth, but rather as a spotlight searching my soul. It tore into corners of my interior making visible things I had long kept hidden and thus could pretend did not exist. It showed me how I had ignored or willfully acted in ways contrary to what I knew was right. More surprisingly, the Light made visible how thoroughly I was loved and made clear that I was worthy to speak, in stark contrast to my own habit of denigrating myself. I could fight it off, but ultimately I could not escape the message of the Light to stop believing the voices from my childhood that told me I had nothing to say and to listen instead to the Inward Guide.

For my spiritual ancestors, that Light was available to every heart, opening up the painful, dirty corners or, as Thomas Hamm, Professor of History and Curator of the Quaker Collection at Earlham College, recently said on Facebook, the Light reveals our 'spiritual dust bunnies' and all the odd corners. The Light then gives guidance how best to use the broom to sweep out the corners. It shows us how to enjoy and value our being and engage anew with the world. This was part of the power of the Light, the Light which ultimately leads into healing, growth and wholeness. The work of the Light is not the property of a special, chosen few, but present for all who accept it and move with the changes it makes possible.

I wonder about the ways in which an Eskimo or a Greenlander views sunlight and darkness when the dark so completely swallows the sun each year in the Arctic. How much of a threat is the sun to someone caught on the desert dunes in mid-summer? The flowers of alpine buttercups and other heliotropic plants turn to always face the sun, cacti have ways of protecting water from fierce sunlight and drawing it out of apparently barren lands, blooming rapidly at the onset of rain. What is it in the human soul that seeks the holy Light like these buttercups? How do we change our actions in response to the fullness of the tropical sun? How do we learn to treasure the memory of the fading sun in the Arctic winter and have faith that it will return?

The natural world offers us many images of change. Genetic change or geological shifts require millennia or more. Yet startling change can happen within a lifetime that may only last a few weeks such as the emergence of the butterfly from its chrysalis where massive transformation has invisibly occurred. These are good reminders of how varied our experience can be and how important discernment can be. We, as humans, have constant pressures on us during our lives to shift our behavior and hearts in one way or another, not all healthy for us as individuals or as part of an ecosystem. Awareness of direction that is of the Spirit and that which is cultural pressure or some other force pressing towards revenge, or over-consumption, or any number of other ways we can go astray is central to the spiritual condition.

Discernment and transformation are both integral to prophetic ministry. Both are topics I often write about and teach, so I find myself bumping into yet another point where something has to give. Emotions, intellect and soul rub up against each other uncomfortably, and in me often do so until a shift occurs. Reaching a new point of reconciliation between self and God in a way that brings to mind the old Quaker saying 'Live up to the measure of Light thou hast and thou wilt be given more'. Another distinctive way Quakers once talked about this is in terms of growing into perfection—perfect obedience to the Light of Christ, completion, wholeness. The very idea of perfection keeps re-engaging me as I wonder what wholeness might be like in my own life and in our Meetings. I do know that as we grow, this place of perfection shifts and we are transformed yet again as another dark place in the soul is lit up and filled with Life.

The way to recognising and naming a ministry is not always simple or obvious as Carla Coleman (Northwest Yearly Meeting of Friends Church) has found.

> I was always super sensitive ... to everyone and everything. I was the one who thought I saw around issues, found another way, or stood up to conflict when people around me seemed to be asleep, not that this has happened often. Through many years of personal healing and forgiveness I finally began the journey towards God's love. He's been closely walking besides me teaching me about His love and what it means and costs to love like Him. When I sense God's heart, and if I'm aligned with Him, I know when something goes against God's loving heart. Naturally, that only happens if I am centered in Him. [3]

A few people experience a moment when life changes. It may be a major shift, perhaps a calling from God to take up a ministry or a decision to stop using alcohol. It may be a simple one as when I woke from a dream aware I had to stop drinking multiple cups of coffee each day. But even such instantaneous shifts are not the whole story. Those of us who experience sharp, unmistakable moments of turning find that translating that into daily life takes patience, commitment, greatly aided by those who walk alongside us. Early Friends, in their journals, would speak of 'many baptisms'—multiple times when the Spirit was strong in them and orientated them closer toward God. 'Conviction' was also an important word for them—in the Light of Christ a person was convicted of sin (which may only have been that they loved to dance, something we would definitely not label a sin today), but most importantly, the Light would show them the way to live in the Truth. These early Friends were quite vocal about the Puritans and others who did not believe we could live in this state free of sin and accused them of 'preaching up sin'.

The modern concept of coming into wholeness is one translation of the Greek word *teleios* which is used by Jesus in the Sermon on the Mount. Right now I like the alternate meaning of 'undivided'. This gives me the hope of not being internally torn between competing pressures and desires. I experience moments when I am focused on my writing in a way that includes attention to those who might read my work and to the inner voice that opens me to a sense of purpose greater than my own. When this happens, I find myself deeply engaged in a manner that leaves me feeling light, feeling that I am for at least this time walking in the Light.

Recognising and supporting ministry

Living in this world is a demanding task for many of us. It takes all our energy and attention just to get through the day, to earn enough to nourish our bodies and those of our families, much less paying attention to the Spirit. The press of the here and now is real and demanding. We may hardly recognise when our lives have slipped into constant activity that has little to do with the values we hold most dear.

Yet, even in the rush of obligations, the deepest hope of our hearts might glimmer through. Dorsey Green of the liberal, unprogrammed, North Pacific Yearly Meeting calls attention to the times we may be doing God's work without any awareness of calling or even conscious decision-making.

> I actually suspect that many people are called to and act on that call without recognising it for what it is. I think most of us need to pay a lot of attention and listen for divine direction. The world is so busy and fast that I certainly can go a long time before I realise I'm not listening or grounded. [4]

I know I need practice, and external reminders to remember to still my mind enough to let go of the internal commentary and my tendency to pronounce judgment on everything, especially my own behavior. In the constant chatter there is almost no room for the Inward Guide to get in a word edgewise.

Some people actively yearn for that spiritual guide and a sense of holy direction for their lives. As someone who spent over half my life with no inkling that I might possibly have a ministry, or even be open to hearing the Spirit present in my life, I am all too aware how unexpected a divine calling is for some of us.

The call may be gentle and simple, only requiring us to act for a moment or in small, private actions. To listen for and respond to such calls is at the core of being an everyday prophet. At times, the call may be to broader, more visible work, the work of the radical prophet, the Public Friend. Such Friends flourish amid supportive communities that carry the vision of prophetic ministry and living into the New Creation.

Programmed/Christian Friends not only expect change: conversion in some form. They expect some individuals will be called to a particular ministry, usually a ministry of preaching and offering pastoral care that will be supported financially when the person takes up pastoral leadership. Such Friends are normally formally recognised by their Monthly or Yearly Meeting by being recorded as ministers. The recording process may include seminary, but historically the process has been a period of study and reflection under the care of Elders of the Meeting. In addition, the Elders and the various Yearly Meeting Superintendents have responsibility for holding the minister accountable and for offering spiritual and emotional support.

In the unprogrammed, liberal Meetings, only a few formally record the gift of ministry. In these Meetings, the recording process came close to dying out completely in the early 20th century as it became seen as a block to the free flow of the Spirit in the Meetings. In recent decades, recording a gift in vocal ministry is being revived in a few places such as New England. More often Meetings are taking up the process of recognising individuals who are called to a particular ministry, perhaps in social justice work, perhaps in care for aging and dying, etc, usually for a specified time. These Meetings minute that the Friend is released for that work and care is given in the form of a Support Committee and a requirement that they report back regularly to the whole community. At times, the individual is also reimbursed for travel or other direct expenses.

Taking up the cross: the power

Against all rationality, the fact of letting go of something dear, of releasing the need to control one's life, of admitting personal powerlessness, can be the point of transition into strength. Margaret Fell, in 1660 wrote of 'the cross of Christ, which is the power of God'. [5] She knew that only by standing in this place of the Cross, affirming in the Garden of Gethesmane that 'thy will be done', only in this is the power to embody the City of God and make it a reality.

I have recognised this in others. Some of the more visible, publicly recognised instances have been in releasing the hold of alcohol or other addictions. One example is Rachel Cunliffe (formerly Hardesty), member of North Pacific Yearly Meeting (independent, liberal, unprogrammed) and a professor in Criminology and the Criminal Justice System at Portland State University. Her work has been formally recognised by her monthly meeting.

She found that divine intervention could stop the urge to medicate past hurts with alcohol and drugs. Once addictions lost their control over her, her life became devoted to service to others. She describes her ministry as follows:

> My work has been in the context of a compassionate listening project with people entangled in the death penalty. It has undergone various evolutions in the now, nearly 21 years since it started. Currently, I consult with defense attorneys on capital cases [which result in the death penalty] to try to develop what opportunities there are for restorative justice capacity building. This frequently brings me in contact with the survivors of people who have been murdered with opportunities to help them achieve a measure of restorative justice alongside criminal justice processes.
>
> During one evolution of the listening project, I was very involved in advocacy and activism around the death penalty specifically. That was when Multnomah Friends Meeting took my ministry under its care. Since then, my focus has been more on building peace and reconciliation among those who have been affected by a murder. This is not to say that I believe that they must reconcile with each other, but, much in the vein of Murder Victims Families for Reconciliation, I believe that we must all face our histories and come to some kind of reconciliation with them if we are to reclaim our lives from the past, and live in the present.[6]

There are infinite variations of the listening and the turning that are inherent in the concept of taking up the cross. The lives of many people like Rachel witness to another way of being where we pay attention to that Inward Light that points to justice and reveals our part in it.

The idea of 'taking up the cross' is sometimes used to claim a need for us to suffer as Christ did in order to become more like him. The early Quakers did not use suffering as their measure, but rather obedience. To take up the cross is to listen to the divine call, not our personal, immediate desires. When it means we have to give up whatever is most appealing to us at the moment, or let go of our personal comforts, there may be times of suffering. But that is not the point. As so many have attested, this place of obedience has not only meant greater freedom, compassion and equity, but also surprising joy and a sense of rightness deep within.

Jean Zaru, the activist Quaker leader, writes from Ramallah, Palestine of the ongoing change in the human heart when the Spirit of Christ works amid the suffering and pain of so many venues and communities that have been torn by aggression and hatred. Immersion in the reality of such places raises up impossible seeming questions whose answers are beyond conventional human solutions.

> We are called to conversion, to be converted to the struggle of women and men everywhere who have no way to escape the unending fatigue of their labor and the daily denial of their human rights and human worth. We must let our hearts be moved by the anguish and suffering of our sisters and brothers throughout the world. How can we bear the pain, and where do we look for hope? Is there anything we can do to solve the political chaos and crisis in the world? Is there anything we can do to stop wars of all kinds? [7]

As in the case of those who hold up Christian conversion and salvation through Jesus Christ as central, there are Friends worldwide who see the turning point in acceptance of responsibility to lift up the poor and suffering, to end violence and to live simply.

Walking humbly and serving boldly

What the lives of other Friends tell me is that transformation in some manner is central to all of us even while it is a point of serious contention. Turning, awakening, being transformed, recognising that we cannot do it all on our own without an Inward Teacher: these are all part of who we are. Among the most widely quoted of early Quaker writings are Isaac Penington's words from his work:

> Give over thine own willing; give over thine own running; give over thine own desiring to know or to be any thing, and sink down to the seed which God sows in the heart, and let that grow in thee, and be in thee, and breathe in thee, and act in thee, and thou shalt find by sweet

experience that the Lord knows that, and loves and owns that, and will lead it to the inheritance of life, which is his portion. [8]

These words encompass for me the paradox of knowing that the one true Inward Guide is Jesus and knowing that the Inward Guide is a force of love and truth in the world that can guide every individual no matter what their beliefs or religious tradition. Penington would say both these things are true. Without question Christ was his Guide, yet he measured following the Guide by the evidence of a person's actions and words. Today, we have held these out as separate criteria.

No matter how one names the Inward Guide, for this to be a true Guide, we must be called 'to do justice, and to love kindness, and to walk humbly with your God' (Micah 6.8) This Inward Teacher can show us how we might live more humbly, knowing that we are no better (and no worse) at the core than others around us.

We have no special right to wealth or privilege, no special claim to think that everything we have to say, even in worship, has merit. At the same time, when we have spent time in discernment and know the motion of the Spirit in our lives, we have the responsibility to speak what we know boldly.

What then does it mean to walk humbly?

Be grounded, without pretence.

Be fertile soil for the growth of the Spirit among us as humus is for our gardens.

Know that I am neither more nor less worthy of being called by God.

Know that I am loved of God, as are all people.

Live with an undivided heart.

Be teachable.

Be open to the unexpected.

Walk with God.

Listen and Follow.

The importance of humility is recognised among Friends worldwide. The day I wrote this, John Muhanji, Friends United Meeting Mission Director in Kenya posted the following on Facebook:

Why is humility a strong Quaker value? Humility is the true key to success. Successful people lose their way at times, as some Quakers did in the past. They often embrace and overindulge from the fruits of success. Humility halts this arrogance and self-indulging trap. Humble people share the credit and wealth, remaining focused and hungry to continue the journey of success. Share what you have to promote the ministry of Christ. [9]

How might we better serve boldly? So often being bold gets tangled up with aggression and anger. Such attacks often contribute instead to adversarial situations and cut off the possibility of problem solving and developing relationships. Following are some ways that being a Quaker is gradually teaching me about living boldly:

Start in prayer.

Do Truth—live in that power of Life that takes away the occasion for war.

Be passionate. Act out of the courage that comes with faithfulness to the Spirit.

Act with clarity—see beneath the words.

Seek a just peace.

Empower others—don't just assume what they want and need.

Listen with respect for the Divine spark in each heart,

Be accurate and speak truthfully,

Be transparent.

Be willing to have your words and actions tested.

Know when anger energises you to act and when it is pressing towards destruction.

Act with kindness rather than just being nice.

Act with the confidence that comes of knowing the Inward Guide,

Stop thinking you have to defend or apologise for being faithful.

Live in a state of teachable assurance.

Always be grounded in compassion. Know deep joy.

Constantly pray for guidance.

Speaking up. Being bold. These are among the hardest actions for me. I do not talk easily and strongly dislike anything that might call attention to myself. Thus, to speak boldly is a critical spiritual discipline for me. How can I notice when I should be doing this? I too often notice well after the fact and am embarrassed. Can I find ways to make amends for when I am wrongly silent? Such are dimensions of this spiritual discipline in my life.

Liberal Friends often joke about being introverts, so I am clearly not alone in needing to practise being bolder. For others the challenge may be more along the lines of recognising when speaking firmly slides over into hostility towards others, or gets tied up in anger or judgement and becomes destructive. This is all part of staying in touch with the Inward Teacher which can keep our lives in balance so we might better build up our communities and find ways to strengthen them rather than berating them.

Being a Friend often calls us into living amid paradoxes. Not only are we asked to walk humbly and serve boldly, but also to take personal responsibility even as we live out of God's Grace. A challenge for us today is to define a clear group identity for ourselves as Friends and at the same time be radically inclusive. Many more such paradoxes exist. When we, as human beings, set such issues up in opposition to each other, they polarise us and cause us to reject one another, or even demonise each other. Grace abounds when we can recognise the paradox as such rather than assuming the worst or projecting our fears onto those with different beliefs.

This brings me back to discernment, the skill of being able to recognise what is truly damaging and needs to be changed and sort that out from what is simply uncomfortable or outside our experience. George Fox was adamant about knowing one's own inner state so that we can see when we are the problem—today we would talk about not projecting our own fears and other problems onto the situation around us. Fear is the strongest inner headwind in my life and it often interferes with my ability to act. It is up to each person to be able to name what is true for them and find ways to warn themselves when such winds arise.

One modern caution I would raise is in the way we sometimes use the phrase 'way will open', as if expecting that in being called to an action, everything will go smoothly. At the spiritual level that will be true when we are clear as to a leading. However, we may find ourselves at odds with our Meeting community or others we expect to support us.

Such a situation opens up possibilities for testing to see if the leading is true, but it may also mean that we have touched on an uncomfortable issue which requires others to change. In which case patience and gentle persistence may be needed. Certainly, when working in the world, perhaps against those who are doing violence, resistance and angry response may well be firm signs of being on track. Being aware of and exploring our own responses to such headwinds is an important part of prophetic ministry.

Headwinds

In this world obstacles are frequent, be they unexpected ice storms or abrupt encounters of predators and prey. In our human communities, following the Inward Guide opens the way we are to go, but does not necessarily mean our path will be free of obstacles. When strong headwinds arise humans too often seek to overpower them, making bigger and better engines to fight the wind. The nature of ministry is to take a different way, to work with the headwinds as experienced sailors do, knowing a divine power protecting and guiding at all times. The headwinds may rise out of personal fears, or reflect a community that seeks the comforts of the world as its primary aim, or any other of the seemingly infinite ways we hurt one another and resist taking on the risks of change even when we can see the rightness of a new way of engaging with the world. The prophet, be it the everyday prophet, the radical prophet or the prophetic community, has no assurance of success beyond faithfulness and faith that their witness will be noticed amid the violence of society.

Anyone who has taken the helm of a sailboat for any length of time knows viscerally the wind blowing right in your face that pushes you to a stop or even backwards if you attempt to steer directly into its full force. Tacking—the art of using the energy of that headwind but at an angle so it still propels you ahead—is integral to any sailor's skill set. Done well, it can move the boat swiftly and smoothly in the direction you are headed. Your course will not be a neat, straight line, but rather seem to take you to one side or the other. Learning when to come about and head in another direction is essential in keeping off the rocks.

Headwinds come in many forms. Resistance may be invisible, at the level of spirit, and may arise, due to unspoken resistance from those around you, as Ken and Katharine Jacobsen, elders of Ohio Yearly Meeting (Conservative) describe below. Yet resistance is frequently active, made visible in sharp words others speak or their refusal to support an individual ministry such as Margaret Musalia describes below. Alternatively, the headwinds may be internal, including from fear, a sense of inadequacy or even pride. Any of these winds can block us from proceeding unless we recognise them and find the right way to engage them. This chapter will consider the external headwinds: the ways the community resists ministry in its midst, and the following chapter will address the internal headwinds which may block us even when we are surrounded by those who support us.

Opposing spiritual energies

In worship, Friends are taught to listen, for their own deepest thoughts, hopes and blocks, and beyond that to the message that the Inward Teacher might have for their lives.

In the gathered or covered Meeting for Worship, many of those present can experience the movement of the Spirit that holds the entire group in prayer. Even those without a strong awareness of the Spirit can often feel the embrace of divine caring and guidance. Such a Meeting may feel like a fair wind at the stern which fills the sails and moves the boat forward with stately and sometimes exhilarating speed.

In worship, the Eternal Guide can act in mysterious ways when there is a message for the whole community. I first experienced this on a day when I had a clear message I was supposed to speak into the worship, but was held back by fear. Once I stopped fighting—in recognition I was not able to make myself speak—someone nearby stood and gave that message almost word for word. Over the years I have heard many such examples of the Spirit permeating the group and reaching out in ways that defy rationality.

In the silence of worship, there are also times when an invisible force, perhaps from an individual or from the group as a whole, exerts pressure stopping the rise of a holy message. Ken and Katharine Jacobsen of Ohio Yearly Meeting (Conservative) write of this experience:

> I do know that sometimes I sense a great deal of resistance, of headwind, to what I am saying or even to what I am about to say, as if someone/something in the room doesn't want to hear it—but, because it seems right to speak, I am given some strength to keep speaking through the emotional headwind, loud, clear enough to be heard. At

such times of resistance (and I could tell many stories here), when the community or members of it are opposing me, I lose the sense of the 'prophetic community,' a body participating in bearing prophecy to the world. [10]

There is a skill in sensing the different currents moving during worship, a skill that can grow with practice. Even as I assert this, I also know how hard it can be to be aware of the spiritual dimensions of silence. For much of my adult life I was not conscious of this movement that permeates hearts and souls. When I did come to know it, the revelation was that of coming into an entirely new dimension of experience. The reality that some, or many, of those present in Meeting for Worship cannot recognise the spiritual wind means that many 'deckhands' are operating blind and thus not conscious of the presence of such resistance.

When this happens, the Jacobsens note, the individual can feel quite alone. Yet, when a message is rightly heard by the minister, that individual is often given the strength to continue speaking despite feeling the harsh winds.

> He/she is alone precisely because his/her faith community has abandoned the new and living way to which God always calls them. And when the Quaker community abandons this new and living way (which can and does happen, as you so well know, in subtle and obvious ways), they too make of the faithful vocal minister a 'lone prophet' fighting a headwind rather than a member of the prophetic community bringing to all the fresh winds of the Spirit. [11]

This situation was familiar to our spiritual ancestors. For instance, Isaac Penington tells us: 'When the life is at any time lost, the only way of recovery is by retiring to the invisible, and keeping there, and growing up there.'[12] This, to me, is another way of reminding me to learn the feel of the wind in the sails rather than give in to discouragement or anger.

It is the task of the prophetic minister to listen closely so that he or she might be able to accurately sort out the source of energy and words so that they might continue to name the right course for the community. This requires an ongoing practice of listening and paying attention to the motions of the Spirit day-to-day and a willingness to be a student of the Eternal Teacher, knowing that the more skilled one becomes, the more one is able to take on.

Loud and visible winds

Opposition can arise in any community no matter how progressive and open we think we are (or how true to biblical teachings we think we live, depending on our tradition) even if we see ourselves in a Meeting whose beliefs reflect our own. The timing and issues will be distinctive to each situation, but the reaction to anyone who names the flaws or makes visible the hurts that have been ignored is all too often deadening.

Fighting into such winds is exhausting. Sailing directly into a strong headwind will at best leave the boat stopped. It may be pushed backwards. Or, if the sails are set wrongly, the boat can be tossed around or overturned. Surprisingly, even a seemingly fair wind from behind that moves the boat quickly in the course that has been set, can suddenly become threatening if the wind suddenly shifts or is too strong.

When visiting among Kenyan Friends I heard many stories of the ways in which Friends resisted the ministry of the women among them. It was only in recent decades that Friends Theological College in Kaimosi admitted women and these women found doubt and even hostility to their presence. Theirs has been an experience comparable to the struggle women in the U.S. have faced, only the timing is different and the specific forces of opposition take somewhat different forms. But 2,000 years after Priscilla and other women of Jesus' time were accepted as leaders in the early church women still find those who want to keep prophetic ministry as the province of men only.

Margaret Namikoye Musalia (Ngoya), a pastor in Nairobi Yearly Meeting clearly states that a prophet is one who speaks for God through the Holy Spirit yet she knows the prophet is not always heard in their own church. She offers a sense of the opposition she has felt in resistance to her call to prophetic ministry.

> At my early life as a Christian, God spoke to me clearly and as I mentioned things through prayers, songs, and even talking. I was blocked by the church members. Even if the prophetic message came true later and those who opposed me could still confirm that it was true that the prophetic message came through Pastor Musalia there was opposition. But fear of unknown in Quaker church blocks many good true prophets. These are evil days; the truth and lies are the same.

> I was blocked from doing work by those in Authority; spiritual, mental, material and moral support. Loose talk was used against me: can something good come from Jerusalem?
> If the prophetic comes from God it will stay but not from man. [13]

Margaret's story evokes in me the loneliness of the prophet. The isolation a person can feel in the community that raised them when the Holy Spirit calls to a life which seems alien or threatening to the church even when our tradition supports the message she was given, in this case the right and necessity of women offering ministry when called to do so by God.

What will the neighbours say?

The pressure from our various communities—the neighbourhood, our families, our workplace—can readily push on any of us and make us hesitate to act. These headwinds may be awareness that they will not approve, the potential that we might lose a good job, or the possibility of alienation from family. Arthur Roberts of Northwest Yearly Meeting of Friends Church, author, retired professor at George Fox University and pastor, tells this story from his youth:

> ... an occasion arose that challenged me to 'speak truth to power'. In 1950 *de facto* segregation marked cities, including ours. When a family of colour moved into our neighbourhood, upset residents held a community meeting, using our meetinghouse, to strategise a response. Should I attend? Should I be silent? Should I speak? I pondered how 'block busting' strategies by realtors would probably lead to diminishment—even demise—of our meeting ... Silence seemed prudent. Or should I speak up for racial integration? Nudged by the Spirit I chose to do so. So in the meeting, nervously, I stood up. 'These people are good neighbours', I said, 'I have visited them. The best way to preserve our community is to welcome this family among us and continue to enjoy our homes.' At this point I was booed, and leaders of the gathering requested that local elders fire me. A few days later the elders met with me. They were caught between pragmatic considerations and Gospel truth. But, somewhat nervously, they affirmed that I had been faithful to Biblical truth. A few days later a neighbour told me, 'After what you said I visited with that new family, and, yes, they are good neighbours.' She thanked me for speaking up. Within a few years the Friends meeting closed as the neighbourhood

changed. Sometimes it is difficult to take principled action in the face of probable and unwanted pragmatic consequences. But perhaps my faithfulness to truth led to personal choices by others who affirmed Christian principles that in the long run led to greater positive good. [14]

Being a prophet means to be open to the leadings of the Inward Guide, rather than limited by our own feelings of discomfort or inadequacy. The Light of Christ may call us into actions which terrify us or ask us to take risks. Fear is sometimes a guide for me: there is a certain quality of fear that indicates, 'Yes! You are to say this!' When I can follow that leading, I gain a deep sense of peace. The prophetic demands we pay attention every day listening for that voice within and to act with courage in response.

The call to change hearts

My Meeting, which now considers itself open and welcoming to gay, lesbian and transgender people, generated many contradictory and shifting winds, especially in the 1980s, in the face of Friend and activist Bonnie Tinker's efforts to convince us that prejudice against gays and lesbians was alive and painfully visible among us. [15] She had a message for us and asked in many ways for us to change and to help change the wider society.

At times the truth of her message was recognised. At times we felt pushed too hard and fought back. We could not change at the speed she wanted us to.

The engagement was erratic and prolonged. The conflicted feelings resulted in the Meeting minuting our support of her ministry but refusing to provide direct financial support for her work. Her insistence that we should marry all couples on the same basis without regard to gender caused us to stop marrying anyone for several years and there are still those who have not forgiven this. The conflicting feelings led to business meetings where many people spoke out of bitterness and agony, causing more hurt. The process was neither clear nor simple. And we were by no means the only Meeting to resist the request of the gays and lesbians among us to be treated as equals in their full selves.

The radical prophetic message was at times not welcomed by us even as more and more of us came to agree the message was rightly given. It also raised the dilemma that changing hearts can take time and hard work even when injustice calls for immediate response. The beauty and weakness of seeking unity, rather than a quick vote with a majority winning, is in this dilemma. Those who disagree can't be ignored and told to shape up. The desire is that all be brought into at least a recognition that the Spirit is at work even if they cannot come to fully agree with the outcome. At times, there are a few who cannot see the underlying unity even when it is widely accepted and find they may decide to leave the community.

A community of everyday prophets can help sustain and grow the more radical prophets among them. Many an everyday prophet is led to offer comfort and articulate hope in various quiet ways. Some individuals are given messages that shake up the practices of their Meeting, a few share an often painful message meant for the wider world. The latter may be readily supported by the Meeting whereas those who offer a direct challenge to Friends may well encounter an angry or hostile response, or can split the community as so many Meetings in the U.S. have found when addressing same gender marriage.

Becky Ankeny, lifelong Quaker and first woman Superintendent of Northwest Yearly Meeting of Friends Church speaks to the risk involved in the ministry:

> … there is also the sense of risk involved in a prophetic ministry—maybe a part of the definition, even—is there some risk to you in what you share? There is little risk (I would think) in insisting that God is love, though I have found that for some, God's wrath is a part of orthodoxy in a way I am surprised by. So there is the risk of being labeled and losing one's voice in the conversation because of not being adequately orthodox.
>
> The prophet seems always to be resisted by someone, and when that someone is influential, the resistance can be lethal to the prophet. The prophet often confronts the complacency of those who define what God wants as a series of criteria and urges them instead to live in dynamic and obedient relationship with God. [16]

This is part of the preparation of the prophet: recognition of the likelihood they will not be well received, certainly not among those whose fears and greed they are exposing, but perhaps even in their home community. When we come to that recognition, can we also learn to ask 'Where do I find support when these headwinds arise?' and 'What are my own weaknesses that if not addressed will cause me to steer off course, to fail in my faithfulness?'

Finding one's rightful place

As I hear people tell their stories of faith and the manner in which they found the work that was theirs to do, I am struck by the infinite ways love moulds the heart and frees the soul. I am one of those who happen to be able to point to a moment in time when all things were new, yet I also carry a tale of stubborn resistance, back-tracking, and long slow opening. For each of us the challenge is to recognise the Still Small Voice and follow it even when it seems to make no sense, or when fear rises up, or when the comfort of what once was lures us to inaction. To be part of a prophetic community is to engage, to take the risk of following the unseen Inward Guide and to encourage others to join in this joyous, painful process of seeking and finding.

Being listened into fuller life

The other day at a meeting of the Anchor Committee that supports me in my work, one member had a miserable cold and refused to shake hands. At which point, Nancy held her hands out, one facing upward, the other down, asking us to do the same so that our palms were a few inches apart. Then she asked us to settle into the silence and notice what was happening in our hands. Each of us could feel a subtle movement—of heat? of energy?—just enough to make real the connection among us and remind us of the presence of the Spirit that links us all.

It takes no money. It requires no prestige or special authority. Yet how many among us, when we honestly search our hearts, have truly been listened to? Or, perhaps more importantly, have listened for the workings of someone else's soul?

A central trait of being a Friend is attention to listening, be it to oneself, or to the others who surround us. I believe this listening has its greatest power when we seek the divine impulse, the movement of the Spirit within, when we attempt to hear the Voice of the Light. I purposefully use this somewhat nonsensical name—the Voice of the Light—to make us more conscious that we are listening not just to the words, or to the actions, although both are integral to the process.

We are also listening for the breath of the Eternal and seeking to catch a glimpse of the power of love in whatever corner it bubbles up.

Part of our challenge is to *feel* the presence of God and the movement of Truth and Love. This is not 'feeling' as in the modern usage, but a deep inward knowing that is more than intellect and emotion. It allows no space for manipulation of others or falsity. When we feel the *inward motion* that comes from God rise up in us, then we are rightly led to speak, be it in worship or in daily life.

Tools for sorting

It is easy, but sometimes painful for me to recall one Friend, who was working hard to open the hearts of the whole meeting community. At various times during business meeting I would sense that she had full support. Then, she would say something harsh or aggravating and we would slip back into contention. Her own insecurities and fears were damaging to the work she was called to do. I know I am not immune to this as it is so easy for me to let my fears dictate what I am willing to say. I am at such times aware of how my all-too-human self doesn't believe that I can do the work God has laid before me. My heart is too often divided.

How do we come to recognise when our self starts to divide us from the leadings of the Spirit? How do we move into a state where our souls are undivided? And. Perhaps more importantly, how does the Meeting community help nurture and strengthen the ministry in its midst?

For twenty years now, ever since Multnomah Meeting formally minuted my ministry of writing and teaching, I have had an Anchor Committee named by the meeting. This committee, which has had several iterations of members over the decades, has the dual purpose of providing spiritual and practical support to me and at the same time holding me accountable and reporting on my work to the meeting. They have read much of what I write, been present at various talks and workshops I've given locally, heard reports back on talks I've given elsewhere. In the initial years, their work was focused very much on reading what I wrote. In more recent years their focus has been on the spiritual dimension, and when they read my material, they seek the movement of the Spirit, not intellectual content.

Being given space to speak to the community, and to my Anchor Committee, has been my greatest teacher as I have gradually come to learn much about myself as well as about being a Friend. By being willing to listen, and to respond truthfully and with vulnerability, such people have taught me much about recognising the motion of the Spirit. I have also benefited much from the workshops and programs offered by others, some sponsored by my Meeting, others at scattered venues. While I have been fortunate enough not to need financial support to attend such gatherings, I know it has been essential to others in the community that we have a fund set up to cover the costs of travel and registration. The benefits are magnified when we push people to offer presentations to the whole community when they return.

Sessions in discernment can never be held too often, it seems. Honing the inward ear is a life-long task, as is learning about one's own strengths and weaknesses and the ways in which we can ask for help when the task seems overwhelming. Because I do so much cross-yearly meeting work, I have learned some about prayer and come to know a bit of what we lose when we ignore its potential. It is still difficult for me to pray aloud, but I have seen how many times this practice has been valuable to others.

Two other practices I would note. One is eldering: eldering in the sense of nurturing and bringing forth ministry in others. Friends have tapped me on the shoulder and asked me to undertake actions which surprised me. Others have sent a simple note thanking me, or making a suggestion. I love the statement of one Friend from Africa who is thankful for criticism because it means they have paid attention enough and care enough to speak up. The gift of eldering may show up in a multitude of ways and unexpected time. We should each be aware of the call to elder those around us.

The other practice is that of clearness groups, support groups and peer groups. Each of these variations is grounded in encouraging individuals to attend to the Holy One and what guidance might be there for us. In a clearness group, an individual is looking for the right response to a particular dilemma or attempting to discern a calling. In a support group, several individuals are aiding the focus person carry out a leading, or respond in a grace-filled way to a complex or hard time in their life. Peer groups offer the opportunity for a few people to meet regularly and give each one equal time to respond to the question 'How is the Spirit with thee, Friend?' then close with a query 'How may we pray for you?'

Many Meetings are not large and often people have little experience with or even knowledge of some of these practices, but resources are available on the web at locations such as the Friends General Conference travelling ministries program. Various larger communities such as Central Philadelphia Monthly Meeting and New England Yearly Meeting have helpful websites. Isaac Penington is one of my most important teachers along with Margaret Fell and other writers of past and present generations. I know from experience that Peer Groups can work among Friends at a distance and have been part of one meeting by phone for several years.

Alternatively, one small Meeting in Wisconsin has formed itself into 2–3 Peer Groups each year and built strong connections within a tiny community. Thus, it may take imagination and persistence for someone seeking spiritual nurture to help create what is needed with the resources available.

Naming and calling forth gifts in others is something that can happen no matter how many are present, although sometimes it is necessary to reach out across distances or generations to find the right elders and peers.

Thus, my answer to where I find support and external guidance lies in the strength of the community that surrounds me. I know from listening to others, that I am extremely fortunate in the Meeting where I happen to belong.

It has been hard at times to ask for or even to know what I needed. At times we have had to seek out ways of interacting new to us. Being surrounded by others—even one other—willing to listen for the Inward Teacher and speak about what they have learned upholds me when I doubt, gives me courage when fear arises and lets me know when I have gotten caught up in my own ego. Our teachers may be in writings, live next door, or live at a distance, yet all share the capacity to sense love present among us. Together we help each other learn to be voices for justice and compassion in the world.

Watered crops

In *Walk Worthy of Your Calling* Peggy Parsons (now Morrison), wrote this about the essential tie between everyday prophets and the community which surrounds and uphold them:

> Quakers say that God calls forth, or ordains ministers, including those whose ministry is public and those who travel in response to their call. All we can or should do is notice and assist these friends, record or release them. This first step is out of our hands, a gift from God to the community, but the second step is ours—we must expectantly look for

this gift. In the early days of Friends it seemed as though ministers sprang up from the earth like watered crops. Now it seems as if this gift is the rare tree emerging from a crevice in the rock. We marvel at its tenacity, but it does not occur to us to apply fertiliser. We would like to offer some suggestions for the preparation of the ground, for recognising the Divine planting, for training, feeding, and tending to the fruit of God. [17]

Peggy Morrison travelled among Friends for many years as a recorded minister and pastor in the evangelical Friends Church which noticed and recognised her calling. Yet she later had a strong call to live out her belief that all should be welcome into our meetings and we should expect the Holy Spirit to appear in even what we think are the most unlikely people.

As a result of this call, she had to lay down her recording and leave her yearly meeting in order to co-found Freedom Friends Church, an independent Friends meeting in Oregon that is both unabashedly Christian and welcoming to people without regard to their sexual orientation or gender identity. In this church, the pastors gently invite all to participate and actively nurture the many voices among them, creating a joyful space and seeking to draw forth divine fruit.

A community in balance

Friends have always seen ourselves as a community apart from the world, even as we engage in the events that shape our lives. Walter Brueggemann, Professor Emeritus of Old Testament, Columbia Theological Seminary, whose book *The Prophetic Imagination* has done much to shape contemporary thinking about the prophetic voice, emphasises the importance of placing obedience to God above obedience to the state and names the alternative, prophetic community as having an important role in calling the rest of humanity to acting justly and with compassion:

- The social purpose of a really transcendent God is to have a court of appeal against the highest courts and orders of society around us.

- The task of prophetic ministry is to nurture, nourish, and evoke a consciousness and perception alternative to the consciousness and perception of the dominant culture around us. [18]

The understanding of God and the vision for the way humanity might exist on this planet then become critical. A God who rewards goodness with riches or an angry, violent, punitive God can be used to justify such behavior on earth. Brueggemann has described the necessity of an alternative community for nurturing the prophetic voice and how it carries the vision that shapes our lives.

- A long and available memory often in song and story

- An available, expressed sense of pain that is owned and recited publicly

- An active sense of hope

- An effective mode of discourse cherished across generations

We have always been weak in the area of song, although that has changed in recent decades: major choral works have been written using the words of Fox and Woolman, then performed by the Leaveners, and several Quaker song books have been published. A great strength has been our habit of passing down written journals documenting the lives of public Friends. In these volumes the generations share their pain as well as their hope and confidence in God at work in the world and the reality of a New Creation made manifest on earth.

Friends hold a vision that it is possible to live together without violence. That humanity, when it is in tune with the Holy, can recognise when they have enough and thrive on that without amassing great wealth or power over others. That true trust in God will be sufficient when we come to rely on divine guidance and treat one another justly, with respect, and with a conviction that all people must also have access to the basics of life.

The sense of what is Holy runs through my work as a thread through many colours of cloth. The needles that weave this thread prick hard when I ignore them. This thread carries the awareness that humanity holds a unique place to do good or ill along with our responsibility to take the needs of the whole of creation into our consideration. In the Bible this thread runs through the visions of Isaiah, the life and words of Jesus to the beauty of the city built on a hill in Revelation. It runs into all the world and all forms of faith.

Historically, this Holy Guide has underpinned Quaker ministry. It highlights the need to find a balance point between justice and compassion, between humility and boldness, between each individual community and all life on this globe. This thread reminds us of the interdependence and the freedom that are essential dimensions of the ecosystem of ministry.

In various meeting houses and art museums, Edward Hicks' paintings of the Peaceable Kingdom convey the image from Isaiah of the lion lying next to the lamb and the small child playing with the poisonous adder. In the distance William Penn stands among the Lenni Lenape people symbolising his honest, peaceful purchase of their lands.

Isaiah's vision is widely associated with the Kingdom of God and in many ways is quite appealing. Yet it is also very much at odds with what we know now of the natural environment, some of which is hard to reconcile with our peace testimony.

For instance, we now know how important key predators are to the balance of nature and that removing them (or their aggressive behavior) leaves watercourses muddy and trampled by herds of deer or elk, and lets some species expand out of control so that all available food is eaten, and otherwise change the environment.

'Cooperation and conflict drive plant and animal adaptation. Species and their habitats thrive as interactive, dynamic systems that are constantly reshaping each other.' According to the conservationist Joe Scott, without the presence of carnivores, snowshoe hares, for instance, overwhelm the capacity of the land to support them. [19]

There are many, many such examples and I am not the biologist who might build a full picture for you. However, if we are to use the natural world as an image for how humans might behave in the New Creation, in an ideal world, there are harsh realities to take into account. Our spiritual ancestors used the Lamb's War as the metaphor to designate their determination to confront evil in the world while only using the weapons that Jesus used: compassion, trust in God, justice, and other tools of non-violence.

Many people today have engaged in efforts to envision how humans might best live on this planet in harmony with God's way and the natural world that sustains us. I am certain we can't move uncritically from examples taken from the wild as we seek images of the world as we want it to be, yet many compelling such images exist and can be valuable. Certainly, all Meeting communities experience both cooperation and conflict.

Living amid community requires that we adapt, often in small ways rather than alteration of our species. Humans have often chosen the role of dominance in response to disagreement, but our faith raises up cooperation. Many people believe that we can learn much from conflict (as opposed to violence) and that we can learn skills that help us shift conflict from being a destructive process to one that aids in growth and new opportunities. How we engage with our families is one such learning system. The Meeting community another. These and other groupings of human beings reveal our resentments as well as our delight, our envies as well as our celebrations. The closer knit a group of individuals the more vulnerable they are to one another, which is at once a strength and an opening for harm, be it intentional or unintentional.

The late Elise Boulding, a North American Quaker social scientist and peace researcher, believed strongly in the creative role of conflict if we can learn what she has called 'conflict maturing'. She identifies the family in its many forms as the place where one learns the 'skills of human relationship' and also how to 'adapt to one's environment'.

She goes on to say, 'Every newly formed household can be seen as a colony of heaven, in which the work of forming new persons is undertaken'. [20]

Can we see our Meetings as such colonies as well, on a one-step larger scale? Essential to conflict maturing is the recognition that pain in relationships can be a sign of growth. 'What stands there is in the hand of God. The letting be of the other is crucial. In the facing of contradiction is growth.' She finds facing this process as essential as the capacity to love in building familial relationships and fostering individuality. [21]

All this hints at the scope of what she called a global civic culture of peace at the core of living out the Peaceable Kingdom on earth.

Being embedded in a community teaches us much about how to relate to other human beings and how to see our place on the globe where we live. In community, we learn ways of responding to disagreements, making decisions when we hold differing understandings about issues that affect us deeply, standing with people when they are overwhelmed by emotions. The vision our community holds about the future, whether we call it the New Creation, the Kingdom of God or any of numerous other names, shapes us and is integral to our witness to the world of how we might come closer to being a community of everyday prophets.

Having seen the beauty of such a vision, Friends have held it up as a reality that can be made manifest on earth. In knowing this vision, it becomes easy to see when the world is out of balance. To name that imbalance, and to take steps to restore it is also the task of the prophet. The radical prophets may do this in quite public arenas, but even more essential is the array of everyday prophets who live out the vision in their schools, their homes, their cities, their nations. Without the body of the faithful who listen for the Light and help others to do the same, the radical prophets are lost and alone.

Moving with the headwinds

An experienced sailor knows about the angles of the winds and the currents, knows that if you head your boat at the correct angle to the headwind and set your sails accordingly, it is possible to sail quickly and freely. Because you are moving at an angle to where you want to be, you will have to readjust the course periodically and reset the sails so that the overall movement is in the right direction. In tight places, when the wind is strong and rocks are nearby, the boat may need to 'come about' quite frequently to adjust to these forces humans do not control.

Thus it can be as we engage one another, not by clashing, but by feeling where the wind is shifting and engaging with it, knowing that interplay which brings us all home.

My journey heads towards the spiritual North Star. At least that is my intent. This small boat I call my body has few defences against the power of the waves. The power of my muscles and my will are readily overwhelmed by the force of an active storm, or even the intensity of day-to-day winds. Much of the time I do not have the option of powering straight ahead to follow that star unless the wind is with me and the currents aren't too strong.

This image I can feel in my bones from having sailed in the Pacific Northwest among the Gulf Islands, in Desolation Sound, off the coast of Alaska and in the open ocean. In such territory there are many narrow places where the wind and current are against you and are more than the capacity of the boat to overcome. The only option is to wait for the winds to change or the tide to turn. Other days it is still and beautiful, but no air is moving to fill the sails. Without a mechanical motor one can only remain at dock or drift on the currents.

I recall vividly one moonlit night with no wind stirring. We had motored out of the Straits of Juan de Fuca dodging freighters which were visible only as a moving line of black between the sea and the thick fog.

We motored all night along the Washington coast under the full moon and cover of stars. The light was bright enough to see the coastal hills several miles away. Come morning, a breeze arose behind us. We could shut off the mechanical propeller and move silently, with a speed that increased as the day progressed. The wind was directly at our stern—a fine tailwind heading us directly for the mouth of the Columbia River, our destination. The whole day was a glorious sleigh ride running down the long ridge of unbroken waves carrying us forward.

Many metaphors exist to convey what we can of the spiritual, unseen powers that shape our lives. Watching birds flying, coming across a nurse log in the old growth forest, playing a musical instrument. The list can be extended a long ways. Such images can give words to convey the work of the Inward Guide—the spiritual North Star—as well as the force, gentle and otherwise, of the spirits which tie us together or press us apart.

The Bible is full of such images speaking of the experience of God as a mother hen, or being as a weaned child on our mother's lap, protected by the Holy One. We might rise up as eagles in our reliance on God. Jesus loved to use parables and the sowing of the seed was a vivid way for him to communicate his message. With such words we might help point out the way and aid others in finding their sea legs or giving them hope

The flight of the hawk on the winds which are the breath of Life is perhaps the most powerful image I carry in my heart of freedom. But I only know that from watching the hawk and sensing what it might have to say.

In contrast, I can feel the sea rising and falling under me, the wind cutting across the deck or gently wafting by. I know something of the tiller and how it can turn the boat to fight the winds, or to let them move us. I am aware that heart, mind, body and soul contribute to the process and that one can gain skill over the years in sensing and learning to move with the winds being respectful of their action while still keeping focus on the guidance of the Inward Light and where it would lead us.

When facing a strong headwind, there is no use cursing it and trying to go directly to your destination no matter what. You will only be blown backwards, perhaps onto the rocks. This is most evident in the small boats I know, but even the largest of our human freighters can find itself caught on a reef or aground in the muck. Such a lovely metaphor for the way humans too often want to engage with those with whom they disagree. We have such an impulse to attack, to contradict, to let others know we have the right answer. We try and bull our way into the headwind and find the push-back harsh and can make no headway.

Approaching the rocks

There was the day the wind was blowing strong. Six of us were on a sail boat headed towards the rocks off the Maine coast at exhilarating speed. We were confident in our ability to steer this boat and have it 'come about': to turn away from the shore and begin the next leg of the journey we were on.

As we approached the rocks about to make this move that would take us back out to sea, there was a loud ripping sound. The Jenny, the large sail on the front of our boat, tore raggedly in two. This turn was not going to happen as we planned.

Our skipper headed the boat directly into the wind so that the wind was no longer pushing us as hard towards the rocks. The most agile among us clambered over the rigging and took down the shreds of the old sail and rigged a new one.

We can train and practise, hone our skills. We can memorise our most central texts, be they the Bible or the sailing manual. But there is the moment when the sail rips to shreds. The moment when everything we thought would happen, when all our apparent control fails. The moment that when all we can do is to point the boat directly into the wind, the point where motion stops. In that moment of stillness we can begin removing the tatters of expectations and put up the new sail that can once again catch the winds.

The word for wind—*ruah* in Hebrew—is also how the ancients named the Spirit. This same word designates the breath of God and human breath. It speaks of the invisible moving air that can destroy or transport. It is the central force of life. It is an external force that moves us and cannot be held and controlled by mortal hands. This word offers a profound link between Spirit, the breath of life and the wind that constantly circles our planet.

The mystery that is God. The incomprehensible power of the tornado. The breath of life. The spirit that enlivens and nourishes our soul. How do we learn to sail such seas, move amidst such dynamics? We may steer with confidence amid the rocks that can penetrate the hull of our ship, thinking we know how to avoid them all. Then the sail disintegrates in the wind.

When we have attended to the spirit over the years, and learned something of the nature of that divine breath, we can settle back into the stillness with the prow pointed directly into the wind—towards God—and find the way forward. If we panic and flail and get caught up in our own emotions, we may easily be stuck in crisis.

The more we know the ship (our body) and are familiar with the nature of that wind that comes from God, the more we are able to right ourselves and find the course that is ours to follow.

Ministry: Moving before the wind

It seems right to start this closing section on prophetic ministry with an image of crisis. Moving in accord with the wind of the Spirit can be harsh, demanding of all our skills and dependent on our practice and willingness to listen for that sometimes faint breath of life in the midst of chaos.

The motion of the Spirit is sometimes faint, so slight it is easily ignored. The motion of the Spirit is overwhelming and powerful beyond knowing. Learning and relying on this motion of mystery is the way Friends have chosen. The way markers are often invisible to the hardened eye. The voice of the Light is not always heard or believed. Books and charts offer rules and clear direction. Yet without putting hand to tiller in the face of the wind one cannot learn when a sharp motion of the tiller rights the boat and when it spins the craft into the reef. And there may be times when we have done all that is possible and still end up suspended on an uncharted reef.

At times, the foulness of the world rises up in our faces—one image of this is the huge eddy of plastics that many say hovers on the Pacific Ocean, that suffocates fish and mammals that encounter it.

> The trash vortex is an area the size of Texas in the North Pacific in which an estimated six kilos of plastic for every kilo of natural plankton, along with other slow degrading garbage, swirls slowly around like a clock, choked with dead fish, marine mammals, and birds who get snared. Some plastics in the gyre will not break down in the lifetimes of the grandchildren of the people who threw them away. [22]

The inhumanity of human behavior includes using so much that we have no need for and tossing material things thoughtlessly into the world. This is only one of many human actions that make me furious.

At times I get so angry that I can't think clearly at all and simply want to lash out at whoever is acting in such a way..Anger on the open sea is a danger to all on the small floating structure that is keeping us alive and whose sails propel us on our journey. Losing track of where the wind is. Ignoring the gathering billowing dark clouds. Such inattention can easily result in swamping the boat or someone being washed overboard. This reality does not negate the horror of the trash vortex, and in my mind only amplifies the need to take fruitful action.

Attention to God demands that we also attend to the health, the safety of the people and the world around us. This is true in multiple dimensions. Jesus was concerned to heal the body and the soul, the heart and the mind. Jesus also knew that those he healed would not always be grateful, as in the case of the man (John 5) who turned him into the authorities. Yet this did not stop him from healing. Awareness of the winds of the Spirit tells us much about how we might act in response to our own fury at injustice and evil and do so without laying out more harm. Setting the sails with gusto and pressing hard to change what is wrong—both ask us to find the balance between huge energy and the decided calm that lets us read the waves and calculate our course from the stars.

The vast openness into which we sail

To be out under the night sky in a small boat. This is how I best know to describe the infinite. The water and the sky. That is all there is. Depending on the night, the sky may carry its own brilliance of stars beyond naming. The sea may display a phosphorescent wave trailing in our path. The moon may light up mountains along the barely visible coastline. Or the absent moon and stars may leave a different emptiness. The times when the clouds touch the water make the world infinitely finite yet without boundaries or borders.

This is how it is to be totally centered and grounded in God: to be bound in the unceasing distance of all that gives life and awareness. This is where prophetic ministry begins, and returns again and again for substance and renewal.

In this image is also a part of the vision carried by Friends: that of visibility and openness. This is part of our work, to make Truth visible in our lives. The City of God is the city on the hill that cannot be hid, the lighted candle that won't be confined under a basket. The story of the children of Reading is often told, but I never tire of it. When Friends met for worship, the soldiers came and dragged the adults to prison. When other similar groups experienced imprisonment, they only continued to meet in secret. Friends continued to announce the time and place of

Meeting. When all the adults were imprisoned, the children continued to gather in worship at the appointed time and place.

This true tale seems so right for our time and place and speaks to something that may be slipping away from Friends: the willingness to be visible, to not hide. To speak to the power of God in the world and in individual lives is a witness that challenges the State, the government that wants to control its populace and intimidates in the name of safety.

Our meetings and churches serve an important purpose as refuges from the violence of the culture around us. We can be places of protection and healing. Both these functions are so badly needed. But we carry the heritage of willingness to rely on the strength and power of the Infinite to carry us back into society and witness to another way of being that is grounded in beauty, not fear.

Release

Callings to ministry, to prophecy, do not necessarily last forever, or even for a person's lifetime. We reach safe harbour, the end of the voyage or the transition to a new leg of the trip. Attentiveness is needed to know when to lay down such work. The particular work as a whole may be done, or it may be that a given task may be complete. The gift may be withdrawn for some reason. A clear vision may come signaling release as it did for John Woolman who wrote of being released from a task:

> My exercise was heavy, and I was deeply bowed in spirit before the Lord ... At length, feeling my mind released from the burden which I had been under, I took my leave of them in a good degree of satisfaction ... [23]

In this case, Woolman was referring to his attendance at Yearly Meeting and the burden he felt to speak about some weighty Friends who were slave-holders. During the Yearly Meeting he had private conversations with some of these Friends about their slaves, and arranged to meet with all of them after the end of the annual sessions.

Woolman then spoke to them all about the concern he carried and how he had brought them together. He reports 'a free conference upon the subject' after which he felt released from the work. It was only his task to raise this concern and leave it in the hands of individual Friends to listen to the Inward Guide in their own hearts.

The release from ministry or from a particular task may be sharp and clear as it was in this instance with Woolman. It may be a niggling sense of completion, or awareness that someone else has taken up the task, or that health or other demands of life have made it impossible to continue. At times a clearness process for laying down a ministry may be as valuable to the individual and the community as was the clearness committee that aided consideration of taking up the call. It should be honoured similarly.

Arrival in port releases us from the demands of skippering the vessel that carries us, be it a sailboat, a cruise boat or simply our skin and bones. In the harbour there is protection from the heavy winds and seas, opportunity to find fresh food and water, friends old or new to welcome us, dry clothes and much more. Awareness of the need to enter the harbour to find renewal, or even to complete the journey and sell the boat are among the tasks of the prophet.

Being a band of everyday prophets. Is this possible for Friends? Can our communities better be schools for listening and for encouraging faithfulness to the Spirit? I believe so, but it is not an easy task to take up. I believe this is at the core of what we are all about: a faithfulness to the divine Guide that breaks open hearts and remakes them with compassion. People who know the touch of the Light and are willing to follow where it leads, knit together our communities. At the same time, they help make visible when we, and when the world around us, fall short of what we might be even as they demonstrate a different way of living in the world than what the consumer culture values.

Everyday prophets are already part of our communities. We all might be such people. Everyday prophets are at once ordinary and radical, both humble and bold. They act out of a weave of mercy and justice, valuing each being on this earth. Might we cherish those among us who are so faithful.

Endnotes

1. Paul Buckley, editor of works of William Penn and Elias Hicks, member of the liberal, unprogrammed Ohio Valley Yearly Meeting, response to author queries on prophetic ministry, December 26, 2012
2. Samuel Bownas. *A Description of the Qualifications Necessary to a Gospel Minister* (Wallingford, Pa: Pendle Hill Publications, 1989) p. xxvii
3. Carla Coleman, Member of Northwest Yearly Meeting of Friends Church, participant in Way of the Spirit and other cross-yearly meeting activities, response to author queries on prophetic ministry, August 5, 2013
4. Dorsey Green, former clerk of liberal, unprogrammed North Pacific Yearly Meeting and of Friends Committee on National Legislation, response to queries from author, January 30, 2013
5. Terry S. Wallace, 'A True Testimony' in *A Sincere and Constant Love: an Introduction to the work of Margaret Fell* (Richmond, Ind: Friends United Press, 1992) p. 35
6. Rachel Cunliffe, These quotations are her response to queries by the author, October, 2015
7. Jean Zaru, *Occupied with Nonviolence* (Minneapolis: Fortress Press, 2008) p. 68
8. Isaac Penington. 'Some Directions To The Panting Soul'(1661) in *The Works of Isaac Penington* Volume 2, (Glenside, Pa: Quaker Heritage Press, 1995) p. 241
9. John Muhanji, Friends United Meeting Mission Director in Kenya post on Facebook October 14, 2015
10. Ken and Katharine Jacobsen, response to author queries on prophetic ministry, December 1, 2012

11 Ken and Katharine Jacobsen, December 1, 2012
12 R. Melvin Kaiser and Rosemary Moore, *Knowing the Mystery of Life Within* (London: Quaker Books, 2005) p. 139
13 Margaret Namikoye Musalia, pastor in Makadara Friends Church, Nairobi Yearly Meeting, with emphasis on Sunday school, United Society of Friends Women, Kenya, and pastoral care. Also, the first woman in Kenya to be a marriage officer, response to author queries on prophetic ministry, February 18, 2013
14 Arthur Roberts, response to author queries on prophetic ministry, December 18, 2012
15 Constance Grady, 'Remembering Bonnie Tinker', *Friends Journal*, November 1, 2009. www.friendsjournal.org/2009127/, accessed March 28, 2016
16 Becky Ankeny, response to author queries on prophetic ministry, October 30, 2012
17 Margery Post Abbott and Penny Senger Parsons, *Walk Worthy of Your Calling* (Richmond, Ind: Friends United Press, 2004) p. 276
18 Walter Breuggemann, *The Prophetic Imagination*, (Minneapolis: Fortress Press, 2001) p. 23, 5
19 *Conservation Northwest Quarterly*, http://www.conservationnw.org/what-we-do/predators-and-prey/carnivores-predators-and-their-prey, Spring/summer 2011, accessed October 12, 2015
20 Elise Boulding. *One Small Plot of Heaven* (Wallingford, Pa: Pendle Hill Press, 1989) pp. 184-5
21 Boulding, p. 212
22 Greenpeace, http://www.greenpeace.org/international/en/campaigns/oceans/pollution/trash-vortex/. Accessed January 9, 2014
23 Frederick Tolles, ed. *The Journal of John Woolman* (New York: Corinth Books, 1961) p. 118

www.ingramcontent.com/pod-product-compliance
Lightning Source LLC
LaVergne TN
LVHW041310080426
835510LV00009B/944